G000077331

LILLIAN TOO'S
Little Book of
ESSENTIAL FENG SHUI

RIDER

LONDON . SYDNEY . AUCKLAND . JOHANNESBURG

Extracted from Lillian Too's Essential Feng Shui.
First published in 2000 by Rider, an imprint of Ebury Press,
Random House, 20 Vauxhall Bridge Road, London SW1V 2SA
www.randomhouse.co.uk

Random House Australia (Pty) Limited
20 Alfred Street, Milsons Point, Sydney, New South Wales 2061, Australia
Random House New Zealand Limited
18 Poland Road, Glenfield, Auckland 10, New Zealand
Random House South Africa (Pty) Limited
Endulini, 5A Jubilee Road, Parktown 2193, South Africa
The Random House Group Limited Reg. No. 954009

Papers used by Rider are natural, recyclable products made from wood
grown in sustainable forests.
Printed and bound in Denmark by Nørhaven A/S, Viborg

A CIP catalogue record for this book
is available from the British Library

ISBN 0-7126-0067-1

CONTENTS

FENG SHUI FUNDAMENTALS

•

FENG SHUI: THE ART OF HARMONIOUS LIVING

Feng Shui is the art and science of living in harmony and balance with your personal living and workspace by harnessing metaphysical forces – often referred to as chi – in order to create and enjoy great good fortune.

FENG SHUI AS SCIENCE

Feng shui is neither magic nor is it a
spiritual practice requiring faith or
belief in its effectiveness. Rather it is a
system of techniques and methods
based on a very comprehensive set of
guidelines that express the Chinese
view of the Universe.

THE SCIENCE OF ENVIRONMENTAL CHI

Feng shui defines the existence of a life force, chi, in the natural environment which can be either auspicious and accommodating or threatening and lethal. The practice of feng shui is about tapping into the multitude of auspicious energies circulating in the environment and deflecting those that are inauspicious.

THE DRAGON'S COSMIC BREATH

These metaphysical forces, or chi, that float in the air and the space around us are described as the dragon's cosmic breath. The idea is to strive towards surrounding yourself with the maximum amount of auspicious chi.

ACTIVATING LUCK

Feng shui is about consciously
activating excellent harmonious forces
within your personal environment and
living space by knowing about the
cycles of the five elements and about
yin and yang energies.

THE TRINITY OF LUCK

Feng shui is the earth component in
the trinity of heaven, earth and
mankind luck. Heaven luck determines
birth and lifestyle circumstances, while
earth luck comes from living in
harmony with the environment.
Mankind luck is the luck we create for
ourselves by making the most of our
life circumstance.

FENG SHUI WORKS!

When practiced correctly, feng shui always improves your living and work conditions. But it represents only one third of the trinity of luck. If you are not fated to become a big tycoon, feng shui may make you comfortable, even a little rich, but to be seriously wealthy you also need your heaven luck or karma to allow for it.

SUSPEND SCEPTICISM

Suspend your scepticism for a moment
in time and open your mind to discover
another way of looking at the energies
that permeate your environment. Try
some feng shui and experience the
mysterious potency of the living earth's
invisible intangible forces as they
surprise you with a dose of good
fortune.

FENG SHUI AWARENESS

Get used to seeing your environment
with feng shui eyes. Develop a vital
sensitivity to powerful, but invisible,
energies that surround your living
space. In time you will begin to notice
things that you previously took for
granted...like the clutter around you,
or the awful beam above your bed!

IN MODERN FENG SHUI, ORIENTATION IS MOST IMPORTANT

In the old days, the practice of feng shui had to do with the search for auspicious locations. Then, natural contours such as hills and streams featured prominently. Today man-made structures such as roads, buildings and entire cities have made orientations a great deal more important.

EXAMINE THE
EXTERNAL ENVIRONMENT
OF YOUR HOME

The condition and quality of your
exterior feng shui is often more
important than the layout and
decoration of your interiors. The effect
of external structures in a radius of at
least half a mile can often prove so
lethal it can threaten your family's
wellbeing, health and safety.

LOOK IN FRONT, BEHIND
AND ABOVE

Buildings and structures in front
of your main door have the greatest
potential to be damaging. Behind, it is
the lack of land, structures and
buildings that can cause bad feng shui
because then, support is lacking. A
flight path above you creates noise and
turbulence, considered bad feng shui.

THE BEST SITES

The most auspicious type of land is
undulating, with gentle slopes, hills
and valleys, a good mix of sunlight and
shade, and where the wind does not
blow too strong. In such places look for
land where the grass grows green and
there is a flow of water.

AUSPICIOUS ORIENTATIONS REQUIRE THE MOUNTAIN BEHIND

Behind the home, is the place of the
black turtle which offers the protective
energy of strong support. A hill or
mountain behind your home signifies
the precious and protective turtle that
takes care of you and your family.

NEVER CONFRONT THE MOUNTAIN

Your home, or the building that houses
your home if you live in an apartment,
should be oriented so that the main
front door does not open directly
towards a hill or mountain. In a city, a
high wall or a large building is
considered to be a mountain.
Try to avoid such abodes.

OVERCOMING CONFRONTATIONAL FENG SHUI

If your main entrance faces a mountain
or high structure, consider re-
orientating your front door so that the
structure is behind you rather than in
front. In this way you will be tapping
into its protective energies.

Or use another door.

AUSPICIOUS ORIENTATIONS: LAND LEVELS

On the left side of your main door as you look out is the place of the auspicious green dragon, which brings material success: wealth, position, influence and power. Land on this side should be slightly higher than that on the right, which represents the white tiger.

RAISING THE CHI OF THE
DRAGON SIDE

If the tiger side is higher, one solution
is to erect a very tall light on the left,
or dragon, side. Another is to
artificially change the contours by
creating a small hill on the left side.

IN THE CITY

In the city, the building to your left symbolises the green dragon, and it is auspicious if it is slightly higher than your building. The building to your right is the tiger and this should be slightly lower than the dragon side.

BEING LOWER THAN NEIGHBOURING BUILDINGS

If your building is lower than neighbouring buildings, the flow of benevolent chi towards it will be blocked, thereby adversely affecting its feng shui. Correct by putting a light on the top of the building, shining upwards. This lifts chi.

WATER NEAR YOUR HOME

Any natural flow of water, such as
a river, in the vicinity of your home
should always be in front of it and in
full view of the front door. Water
passing behind indicates opportunities
coming your way will stay just out of
reach, and slip away.

WATER ON THE MOUNTAIN

This is one of the major warnings of feng shui. When water reaches its zenith, it overflows, causing grave misfortune. Thus, houses should never have water on the roof level or have blue roofing tiles, as blue symbolises water.

HOMES ON THE HILLSIDE

The most auspicious hillside locations
are at mid-levels, which enjoy good
views of the valley or sea below and the
protection of the peak behind.
Avoid the bottom and especially the
summit, which is exposed to high
winds without protection or support.

AVOID DEAD ENDS

Try to avoid living at the end of a
cul-de-sac. Here chi is said to stagnate
and, should problems arise, bad luck is
magnified as this configuration
symbolizes there is no way out.

STRAIGHT ROADS AND
T-JUNCTIONS

Living in a building that directly faces
an oncoming straight road is regarded
as extremely harmful. The bad chi
which enters your home is lethal.
However this deadly chi cannot reach
homes located higher than the road.

COPING WITH STRAIGHT ROADS AND T-JUNCTIONS

If your house is lower than the road,
you can symbolically raise it by
erecting a tall light behind the house.
The deadly chi of a straight road
opposite your house can be blocked off
with a hedge, a wall, or by planting
some trees.

BASEMENT FLATS

Chi that stays below road level is seldom auspicious, so avoid basement flats unless there is a level garden to compensate. Even so, sleeping below road level causes residents to suffer from stagnating chi which makes success difficult to obtain.

LIVING ON A WINDING
ROAD

A house on the inside of a curve,
embraced by the road, enjoys good feng
shui. But the chi on the outside of the
curve is malevolent. A house located
here suffers bad feng shui as the road
becomes a knife which symbolically
cuts into the house.

FAST-MOVING TRAFFIC

Generally it is not a good idea to live
too close to roads and highways where
the traffic moves exceedingly fast.
Here, like the traffic, chi also moves
much too fast, bringing harmful
misfortune.

SLOW-MOVING TRAFFIC

Slow-moving traffic offers potential
for better feng shui, but roads that are
frequently plagued by traffic jams
cause luck to stall and stagnate.

FLYOVERS

Elevated roadways can cause serious
feng shui problems. If you live too
close to a flyover a good solution is to
try planting some tall trees between
your house and the road. If possible,
you might wish to consider moving out.

SELECTING AND CREATING REGULAR SHAPES

•

AUSPICIOUS SHAPES

Whether viewed as two- or three-dimensional, and from any angle or elevation, auspicious shapes are always regular. Square, round, rectangular and octagonal shapes are considered auspicious. Triangular shapes are not.

REGULAR SHAPES PROVIDE BALANCE AND COMPLETENESS

Essential to good feng shui is the regularity of shape of land sites, buildings and other structures. Symmetry of shape provides balance. Completeness is suggested by the absence of missing corners or sections. This important principle extends to rooms and furniture.

UNLUCKY SHAPES

Viewed from different angles and
elevations, inauspicious shapes tend to
have missing corners or irregular lines
and curves. Triangular shapes and
cross-shaped structures are dangerous.

MISSING CORNERS

When there are missing corners, the luck represented by that corner will likewise be missing. For instance, if the southwest is missing, the luck of romance and marriage is seriously afflicted.

REGULARIZING LAYOUTS

A good solution for missing corners is
to build extensions. A simpler method
is to install a tall light in the apex of a
missing corner or, in the case of a
U-shape, symbolically filling it in.

PROTRUDING CORNERS

Protruding corners or extensions can strengthen and enhance the luck of that corner. Thus an extended southeast corner expands the luck of prosperity.

MISSING OR PROTRUDING CORNERS

You can usually see immediately
whether a corner is missing or
protruding by superimposing a square
or rectangle of the basic shape over
a layout of a building. As a rule
L-shaped layouts have missing corners
whereas bay windows and annexes
represent protruding corners.

IDENTIFYING DIFFERENT
AREAS OF YOUR HOME

Take compass directions from the
centre of your house, then superimpose
a square or rectangular grid divided
into nine equal sectors over a layout of
your home. Where the needle points
north, then the grid lying in that
direction represents the north corner
of your home.

FENG SHUI ANALYSIS

Once you have noted all the eight
directions – north, northeast and so on
– you can proceed with a feng shui
analysis of your home based on the
compass sectors.

The same method can be used for
individual rooms.

THE SOUTHEAST CORNER

The southeast represents wealth luck.
If this corner is missing income will
be reduced.

THE SOUTH CORNER

The south is the place that governs the
luck or reputation of the family, and
especially the patriarch. Activate this
corner and recognition follows.

THE SOUTHWEST CORNER

The southwest corresponds to
relationships. It is also the place of the
matriarch. A missing southwest corner
adversely affects marriage and love
relationships. If the matriarch is the
breadwinner of the house, this is the
best corner to enhance with an earth
object, like crystal.

THE WEST CORNER

The west corner relates to the luck of children. Enhancing this corner with metal wind chimes brings good fortune to the young girls of your family.

THE NORTHWEST CORNER

The northwest represents the patronage
of influential people. It is also the
place of the patriarch. The most serious
missing corner is usually the northwest
since this affects the luck of the
patriarch. A protruding corner here is
desirable.

THE NORTH CORNER

The north corners affect career luck.
Activate the north of the living room
with water to jump start a sagging
career.

THE NORTHEAST CORNER

The northeast is the place of study and
contemplation.

THE EAST CORNER

The east corner is the area associated with health. When this place is afflicted in any way it causes the family to get ill. This is also the place of the eldest son and thus it represents descendents' luck.

ENERGIZING THE FIVE ELEMENTS

•

COMPASS DIRECTIONS AND CORRESPONDING ELEMENTS

According to feng shui, attributes of each of the five elements – fire, water, earth, wood and metal – influence each of the eight compass directions. The easiest method of creating good feng shui is to energise the element of each compass sector.

BALANCE AND HARMONY

The use of element theory in feng shui creates harmony which brings good fortune, but also remember that feng shui is as much about balance as it is about harmony. An excess of any single element is inauspicious. Too much water always drowns, too much fire burns.

FIRE

Fire is the ultimate yang element and fire energy brings success, fame and recognition. An extremely powerful element, fire must always be kept under control. A fireplace in the south, with which the fire element is associated, enhances the luck of fame and reputation.

WATER

An extremely powerful element, water
energy brings wealth. When energized
correctly and in balance with other
energies, water brings riches beyond
one's expectations. The best water
energiser is active yang water.

EARTH

Earth is grounding energy, bringing
harmony and great family happiness.
It is the element that dominates the
southwest, northeast and centre of a
home. Placing a globe, the ultimate
symbol of earth, in any of these sectors
brings excellent good luck.

WOOD

Wood energy brings growth, expansion, advancement and the luck of material success. It also confers excellent descendents' luck on families, being especially beneficial to the sons of the family. Wood is associated with the east and southeast.

METAL

Tapping into the energy of metal,
which is particularly associated with
gold and silver, brings great power and
influence. Metal is associated with the
west and northwest. A tiny golden bell,
wind chime or singing bowl placed in
the northwest is a potent way to attract
influential people into your life.

ENERGIZING THE ELEMENTS

Energizing the luck of different corners
of your home by placing objects there
that symbolize the correct element is a
great way to start practicing feng shui.
So have a bright lamp in the south,
a crystal in the southwest, a horseshoe
in the west, a wind chime in the
northwest, a bowl of water in the north,
a ceramic pot in the northeast,
and a pot plant in the east.

ELEMENT THERAPY WITH COLOURS

Each element is associated with a different colour: green for wood, blue or black for water, red for fire, white for metal, ochre for earth. To energize the south part of your home, for example, use any shade of red for the curtains, carpets or paintings.

AUSPICIOUS COLOUR COMBINATIONS

Green/red: excellent in the south, good in the east and southeast during winter months

Red/yellow: excellent in the southwest and northeast

Yellow/metallic: excellent in the west and northwest

Metallic/blue: excellent in the north

Blue/green: excellent in the east and southeast.

INAUSPICIOUS COLOUR
COMBINATIONS

Red/blue or red/black:
very bad in the south
Red/metallic: very bad in the west
or northwest
Green/yellow: extra harmful in the
southwest and northeast
Yellow/blue: very bad in the north
Green/metallic: extra bad in the east
and southeast.

AUSPICIOUS SHAPE
COMBINATIONS

Triangle added to square in the
southwest and northeast
Square added to circle in the northwest
and west
Rectangle added to triangle
in the south
Wavy added to rectangle in the
southeast and east.

THE PRODUCTIVE
CYCLE OF ELEMENTS

Water is good for wood,
but wood exhausts water.
Wood is good for fire, but fire
exhausts wood.
Fire is good for earth, but
earth exhausts fire.
Earth is good for metal, but metal
exhausts earth.
Metal is good for water, but water
exhausts metal.

USING ELEMENTS
PRODUCTIVELY

To energize the wood element of the
southeast, for example, use a water
feature such as a fountain. But in the
north, where the chi is water you must
avoid a wood feature, such as a plant,
since this will exhaust the water chi.

BALANCING
YIN AND YANG

•

YIN AND YANG

Yin and yang are primordial forces that
possess completely opposing attributes,
yet give existence to one another.
Without yin there is no yang, and vice
versa. Neither is good nor bad of itself
but yin and yang give vital balance to
the living space.

ATTRIBUTES OF YIN
AND YANG

Yin is death, darkness and stillness.

Yang is growth, life, activity.

Yin is female, yang is male.

Yin the moon, yang the sun.

Yin the valley, yang the mountain.

Yin and yang continually interact,

creating change which in turn creates

opportunities. Thus summer, which is

yang, gives way to winter,

which is yin.

BALANCING YIN AND YANG

Yang energy is vibrant and alive, and rooms and houses should allow yang to dominate, but not completely deplete yin. The correct balance of yin and yang depends on what a building is being used for and on what kind of room is being assessed.

YIN AND YANG IN
THE OFFICE

Commercial buildings and shopping
places should be made very yang with
plenty of light, sound and activity.
All this creates an air of positive
energy. In such places the yang energy
brings good business luck.

TOO MUCH YIN IN THE OFFICE CAUSES LETHARGY

Offices with an excess of grey steel cabinets, dark coloured walls and dark silent corners are so quiet and so yin they create lethargic energy. Long corridors with rooms opening off them resembling cells compound excessive yin with harmful killing chi.

A YANG OFFICE BRINGS BETTER LUCK

Yang offices are bright, airy
and clean. The energies are never stale
or stagnant. Boardrooms benefit from
a window view, which brings in light.
Plants and music add to the feeling of
life and activity improving the feng
shui still further. Such offices have
good luck.

YIN AND YANG AT HOME

Your home does not need to be
as yang as a working environment.
Yang should still dominate, but to a
lesser extent, especially in the
bedrooms, which are places of rest and
relaxation that benefit from stronger yin
energies.

THE YIN HOME

If the home is too quiet, especially
during the day when everyone is out at
work or at school, yin energy will
accumulate. Counter this by keeping
pets. The presence of life causes yang
energy to flow. Alternatively keep a
moving light switched on while you are
out at work.

THE EXCESSIVELY
YANG HOME

When hot bright sun shines relentlessly
into the home, when the house is too
noisy, where colours are overpowering
and music blares out, excessive yang
energy is created, causing hot tempers,
a lot of shouting and other symptoms of
too much energy. Reduce this by
introducing blues and darker colours
onto walls.

CHI – THE DRAGON'S COSMIC BREATH

•

CHI, THE MAGICAL LIFE FORCE

The dragon's breath is a symbolic reference to chi, the beneficial energy that is said to swirl around the environment. Described as the magical life force, chi pervades the entire universe.

THE GOAL OF FENG SHUI

The aim of feng shui is to select natural
environments with an abundance of the
cosmic chi, where hilly, undulating
land and slow-moving rivers bring great
good fortune. In such places it is most
desirable to build one's home.

BENEFICIAL CHI
MEANDERS

Beneficial prosperity-bringing chi
always meanders slowly. It never moves
fast, and it never moves in a straight
line. When chi gathers speed it
becomes harmful. Thus structure and
layouts should endeavour to create
meandering rather than straight flows
and pathways.

ACCUMULATING
BENEFICIAL CHI

Chi tends to accumulate and settle in
places where there is a good balance of
yin and yang energy. It requires air to
be fresh and clean. When the
atmosphere becomes excessively damp,
wet, dry or hot, chi becomes stale.
When a place is dirty, chi turns foul.
Bad luck then follows closely.

BENEFICIAL CHI BLOWS
WITH THE WIND

Chi is different from the wind, but it
travels with the wind. It exists in the
air, under the ground, in water and in
the human body.

Good chi always brings a feeling of
wellbeing. When this feeling is blocked
it reflects a blockage in the
environment.

BENEFICIAL CHI BRINGS ALL MANNER OF GOOD LUCK

Beneficial chi is vibrant, energetic, full of vigour and the bringer of good fortune. Human chi is the life force which gives strength to athletes and creative skills to artists.
The secret of many Chinese practices and skills lies in harnessing the chi.

ENSURE CHI CAN
FLOW FREELY

Chi which flows around a home should
not get blocked. If, for example, drains
get blocked, the luck of the family
suffers. Similarly Chinese healing
methods are designed to diagnose and
remove blockages in the flow of chi
within the body.

WATER ATTRACTS CHI

Chi is said to stop and settle each time
it encounters water, which is why water
features are considered auspicious.
Water represents money and its
presence in the home tends to bring
good luck to the front door.

SHAR CHI,
THE KILLING BREATH

Feng shui also addresses the presence
of hostile energies within living
environments. These energies, known
as the killing breath or shar chi, cause
intense bad luck. Shar chi is caused by
structures deemed to be sending out
secret poison arrows in a straight line.

POISON ARROWS

The edges of large buildings, straight
roads, even the triangular roof line of a
neighbour's house – all these send out
the poison arrows which cause hostile
chi. When these arrows directly hit
your front door, they create very bad
luck, which must be deflected using
feng shui cures.

DEFLECTING THE KILLING BREATH

•

SHARP EDGES AND TRIANGULAR ROOF LINES

The most serious poison arrows are caused by the sharp edges of constructions such as high-rise buildings, factories, supermarkets or shopping malls, and by triangular roof lines. They pose the greatest threat if your front door directly faces them.

COUNTERING POISON
ARROWS

The best way to deflect these secret
arrows is to create a barrier to shield
your house from bad energy. A clump
of big trees is an excellent cure. Poison
arrows created by the triangular roof
lines of small houses can be deflected
by hanging a pa kua mirror in front of
your door.

LARGE, ELEVATED STRUCTURES

If your front door opens onto a high brick wall, large building, hill or mountain that overwhelms you, the best cure is to close it up and use another door, thereby effectively changing the orientation of your home. Failing that, install a bright light just outside your door.

TRANSMISSION TOWERS AND OTHER HARMFUL STRUCTURES

Structures such as transmission
towers, large chimneys of factories,
telecommication towers, power stations,
bridges and other massive concrete and
steel edifices send out massive doses of
shar chi. Ensure they are behind you
and always plant trees between them
and your home.

HARMFUL JUNCTIONS

T-junctions and Y-junctions are bad
news, especially when a junction
results in a straight road coming
straight at your front door. Build a
barrier of some kind – plant a hedge or
a clump of trees, or build a low wall.

LIVING IN THE VICINITY OF PLACES WITH YIN ENERGY

Living near places with excessive
yin energy – cemeteries, hospitals,
abattoirs, funeral homes and police
stations, for example – is considered
inauspicious. Counter this with a large
dose of yang, for example by painting
your front door yellow, red, white
or orange.

ACCUMULATING
YANG ENERGY

Other effective ways of accumulating
yang energy are to keep your radio
turned on throughout the day, to install
plenty of bright lights, grow lots of
plants, and to keep pets.

GOOD MAINTENANCE GETS
RID OF FOUL BREATH

Peeling paint, defective plumbing and
lighting, dirty polluted drains – such
things suggest stagnant energy and are
the bane of feng shui. The worst form
of foul breath is having your door face
a rubbish heap or garbage can.
Keep your house in good order!

FENG SHUI TOOLS

•

MIRRORS

Mirrors are well known feng shu cures
for example, to correct for missing
corners. But when using mirrors be
sure you do not create more problems
than you solve. Mirrors should never
reflect the front door, a staircase, a
toilet or a bed.

MIRROR TILES

Avoid small mirror tiles. They cause havoc by 'cutting' into people through distorting their reflections. Likewise be sure not to hang any mirror so that the reflection cuts off a part of anyone's head, particularly the head of the family.

PA KUA MIRRORS

The octagonal pa kua shape with a
mirror at the centre is an extremely
powerful feng shui tool. Hung outside
the office or above an entrance door it
deflects a multitude of bad energy and
is especially useful for countering the
killing breath of straight roads,
T-junctions or roof lines.

USING THE PA KUA

The pa kua works by sending out
powerful negative energy of its own to
counter bad energy, so when it is used
to deflect killing chi it may
inadvertently hurt others. It is
absolutely vital that you *never* place the
pa kua inside your home or office.

PLANT THERAPY

Hardy, healthy plants make wonderful
feng shui cures. For example a
creeping plant placed against the sharp
edge of a protruding corner or square
pillar is an effective way of deflecting
the killing breath being emitted. Avoid
plants with thorns or whose leaves
resemble needles.

USING PLANTS WITH CARE

Throw out and replace plants as soon
as they show signs of fading – even the
healthiest of plants cannot live long if
constantly bombarded by the shar chi
of a sharp corner. And never use
plants in a bedroom, where they will
only sap your energy.

BAMBOO STEMS

Bamboo is a potent symbol of
longevity and harmony. Its effect is
similar to that of wind chimes and
flutes. Red string or ribbon tied round
bamboo stems symbolically activates
its channelling properties, encouraging
hostile chi to flow through it and
slow down.

WIND CHIMES

Wind chimes are an excellent and
versatile feng shui tool and many
varieties are available. The rods should
always be hollow and open at both ends
so that chi can be attracted to and
channelled through them, a process
which transforms hostile into
beneficial chi.

CORRECTING FOR MISSING CORNERS OR OVERHANGING BEAMS

Hang a wind chime made of metal in
the east or southeast, of wood in the
northeast or southwest, or a ceramic
wind chime in the north.

ENHANCING THE ENERGY
OF A DIRECTION

If wind chimes are being used to
enhance a direction rather than as a
corrective measure, then hang a wood
wind chime in the east or southeast, a
ceramic wind chime in the northeast
and southwest, a metal wind chime in
the west and northwest.

NOTE THE NUMBER
OF RODS

Wind chimes used to overcome
shar chi should always have five rods.
To *enhance* different corners the
number of rods should be: in the
southwest, two; in the east, three;
southeast, four; northwest, six; west,
seven; northeast, eight; south, nine.

CHANDELIERS

Chandeliers create excellent vibrations
for the home, attracting money and
success luck to each and every member
of the family. Crystal chandeliers bring
even greater luck if they are hung in
fire or earth corners – south, southwest
and northeast – of the home or room.

SCREENS AND DIVIDERS

These make a wonderful corrective
tool for rooms, such as L-rooms, that
are badly shaped. Choose screens that
are decorated with auspicious objects
and display them upright in a straight
line, not in a zigzag fashion which
would create too many edges giving
off shar chi.

HARMONIOUS
LAYOUTS

•

THE FLOW OF CHI

Auspicious homes allow sheng chi
to enter the home unencumbered, and
then to meander slowly from room to
room. The flow of chi is never allowed
to become hostile, nor to stagnate.
Energies are kept vibrant with regular
space-clearing and anti-clutter
maintenance.

THE FRONT DOOR

The main door should not open into
a crammed space directly facing a
toilet, window, staircase, pillar, corner
or a mirror. These taboos should be
observed strictly!

THE LIVING ROOM

The living room should be in the outer
half of the house, nearer to the main
door than the back door. This creates
balance in house layout.

DINING AND FAMILY ROOMS

These should be located in the central
part of the house. This is conducive to
family harmony.

THE KITCHEN

The kitchen should be in the inner half
of the home, and nearer the back door
than the front door.

TOILETS

Toilets should be small and kept closed
at all times. Doors into toilets should
never directly face another door, a
staircase, the bed or the dining table.
Toilets should preferably not be located
in the northwest and southeast of
any home.

THE CORRECT PLACEMENT
OF TOILETS

Main doors, dining tables and work
tables should never be placed directly
under toilets. Toilets in houses with
more than one level should be on top of
each other to safeguard against this
happening.

MULTIPLE STOREYS AND SPLIT LEVELS

If the house has several floors, the dining area should be higher than the living room areas, and sleeping areas should be on the top floor. Multiple level homes are not a problem, but split level homes are considered unbalanced, and liable to result in severe financial loss.

LONG CORRIDORS

There should not be any long corridors
inside the house. They create shar chi,
which leads to quarrels and
misunderstandings in the home.
But long corridors are also conduits of
energy so decorate them in an
attractive way.

STRUCTURAL COLUMNS
AND BEAMS

These should always be flush with the
walls of the house. Exposed structural
beams and corners create massive
shar chi. Try to have them covered.

DOORS AND WINDOWS

Doors and windows should not confront
each other by being placed on opposite
walls, facing each other. This causes
chi to enter and rush out again.

EXTERNAL FEATURES OF A HOME

•

LIGHT UP DRIVEWAYS

Driveways can and should always be enhanced with lights. Keeping a pair of lights on either side of the driveway allows the energy to stay balanced.

DRIVEWAYS SHOULD CURVE TOWARDS THE MAIN DOOR

Driveways should never be straight roads pointing directly at the main door. They should rather curve towards, but not at the door. Circular driveways are regarded as auspicious, particularly those with a fountain in the centre.

GATES

Driveways with a single gate are
preferable to those having two gates,
unless yours is an enormous estate.
Having two gates fronting an average-
sized residential house can give rise to
imbalance and money flowing
outwards.

DRIVEWAYS SHOULD
BE LEVEL

When the drive slopes down steeply
towards the house, this means the
house is below road level, which is
inauspicious. When the drive is
inclined upwards the feng shui is not
so bad, but it is preferable for the
driveway to be level with the outside
approach road.

DRIVEWAYS SHOULD BE
OF EVEN WIDTH

Driveways that narrow inwards or
outwards create imbalance and result
in bad luck. Opportunities cannot ripen
fruitfully and saving becomes
problematic.

FENCES AND GATES

The boundary of the home
demarcates the parameters of energy
that swirls around it. There are
therefore important feng shui
guidelines concerning the levels,
shapes, materials and designs of gates
and fences that should be observed.

FENCES AND GATES SHOULD BE OF EVEN HEIGHT

Any fence around the house should ideally be the same height all the way round, but especially so where it flanks the front gate. If one side of the fence is higher than the other it is out of balance and fortunes may fluctuate and not hold steady.

SOLID FENCES AND GATES ARE GENERALLY BEST

Brick walls and wooden fences are preferable to open fencing such as iron railings or wire netting. However this guideline should be tempered with element analysis which decrees that boundaries on the west, northwest and north should ideally be made of metal.

ORNAMENTAL RAILINGS
AND GRILLES

Anything pointed creates shar chi,
so avoid arrows and spikes altogether
unless they are pointing upward.
Pointing inwards harms you, pointing
outwards harms your neighbours.
Wooden fences and gates should avoid
having crosses or downward
pointing arrows.

THE MAIN DOOR

•

THE IMPORTANCE OF SAFEGUARDING YOUR MAIN DOOR

The main door is of vital importance in feng shui. Get it right, and eighty per cent of your feng shui is assured. On the other hand, if the feng shui of the main door is flawed, the effect is magnified and the bad luck caused is severe.

A TOILET ABOVE THE
MAIN DOOR

A toilet directly above the front door
causes severe bad luck. Change the
location of the door or use another door
as your main door. If this is impossible,
then try to avoid using the toilet and
hang a bright light in the hallway to
clear the bad energy.

A TOILET FACING THE MAIN DOOR

If the front door opens to directly face a toilet, any good fortune entering your home will be flushed away. The best way to handle this is to keep the toilet closed at all times.

THE MAIN DOOR SHOULD NEVER DIRECTLY FACE A STAIRCASE

The best solution to this common but inauspicious arrangement is to create a barrier between the two using a partition or screen. If this is not possible, hang a wind chime in the centre of the wall just above the door on the outside.

THE MAIN DOOR
AND MIRRORS

When a mirror directly faces and
reflects the main door – even at a
distance or from another room – any
good fortune coming into the house
goes straight out again, and the health
of the head of the house is said
to suffer.

CORNERS AND MAIN DOORS

Corners, pillars and sharp edges
directly facing the main door represent
poison arrows that hit the door from
inside the house causing deadly bad
luck. Counter with bushy or creeping
plants placed so as to soften any sharp
edges pointing towards the door.

THREE OR MORE DOORS
IN A STRAIGHT LINE

This is a feng shui taboo, and
considered even more lethal if one is
the front door and one the back.
Create a barrier using a partition or
screen in front of the middle door to
slow down fast flowing chi. Another,
but less effective, solution is to hang
wind chimes or a pair of flutes.

MAIN DOORS AND WINDOWS

Main doors that directly face windows
on the opposite wall have a hard time
holding on to any beneficial chi that
comes into the home. Again, use
screens, wind chimes or a pair of flutes
to correct.

STRUCTURAL FEATURES TO AVOID

•

STRUCTURAL OVERHEAD BEAMS

Heavy exposed beams cause serious damage, sending out shar chi from above onto anyone unfortunate enough to be working, sitting or sleeping beneath them. Either camouflage such beams or move from under them or both. The most effective solution is to install a false ceiling.

ALTERNATIVE CURES
FOR BEAMS

If installing a false ceiling is
unfeasible, soften the edges of the
beams with creeping plants or
decorative frills. In east or southeast
sectors hang a wind chime or curved
knife on the beam. In southwest or
northeast sectors hang a pair of bamboo
stems tied with red ribbon.

PROTRUDING CORNERS

These are as problematic as overhead
beams, though if the sharp edges of the
corners are not directly pointing at your
main door, sleep or working places, you
can escape the killing chi being sent
out by the edges. If you are in the path
of the poison arrows, your luck
will suffer.

CURES FOR CORNERS

Deal with protruding corners by
hanging a large wind chime or hollow
bamboo stems just in front of the edge
of the corner, or by strategically
placing leafy plants to camouflage
sharp edges. Plants should always be
healthy. Avoid plants in the bedroom.

PILLARS AND COLUMNS

Square pillars have the same effect as
protruding corners except that there are
four sharp corners sending out killing
chi instead of one.

Round pillars are not so bad, but still
present an obstacle. Best to cover the
entire pillar with mirrors.

Alternatively use plant therapy.

STAIRCASES

A staircase right in the very centre of
the home represents an injured
household and family unity and luck
are adversely affected. Place a
powerful light at the top of the ceiling
shining down on the staircase and keep
it switched on as much as possible.

SPIRAL STAIRCASES

Avoid spiral staircases. Located in
the middle of the home they are
described as a corkscrew boring into
the heart of the home. If carpeted in
red they are described as the result of
a bleeding heart.

CANTILEVERED
STAIRCASES

Staircases with open, rather than solid,
spaces between them are inauspicious
because luck leaks out even as it
climbs to the upper levels. Always go
for solid staircases, and never carpet
them in red as this is not a good colour
for attracting chi upstairs.

FENG SHUI
DECORATION

•

PICTURES

Paintings of landscapes such as
mountains and rivers are excellent from
a feng shui perspective, especially
when hung correctly so that mountains,
symbolic of support, are behind where
you sit and water views in front.

PAINTINGS THAT INSPIRE

Hang happy paintings that inspire and
that suggest wealth and prosperity.
Paintings of good fortune flowers like
peonies or orchids are auspicious.

PAINTINGS TO AVOID

Avoid abstract art with sharp points
and any paintings which are sad. Also
to be avoided are paintings or prints of
wrinkled old men and women. These
create unhealthy energy.

DO NOT INVITE WILD ANIMALS INTO YOUR HOME

To do so is asking for trouble! Avoid
paintings, prints and statues of wild,
fierce animals. They exude killing
breath. Throw out any souvenirs of big
game hunting: deer antlers and tiger
skin rugs are taboo from a feng shui
perspective.

SOFT FURNISHINGS

Always avoid motifs that are sharp,
angular or threatening. Arrows, points
and triangles are especially dangerous.
Choose instead designs which have
curves and seem to flow. In feng shui
art nouveau is to be preferred over
art deco!

WHERE TO BEGIN

•

FOCUSING YOUR ATTENTION

The major rooms requiring your
attention in terms of feng shui are the
hall where the main door is located, the
living room, the dining room, the
master bedroom and the northwest
corner – that of the patriarch. The
latter should not house the kitchen,
storeroom or toilets.

ENERGIZING THE
LIVING ROOM

Energize the east and southeast with
plants; the south with bright lights; the
southwest and northeast with crystals;
the west and northwest with wind
chimes, bells and anything metallic;
the north, east and southeast with
water features.

THE DINING ROOM

The dining room represents the heart of
the home and should be located at or
near the centre. It should be filled with
yang energy through music, happy
colours and brightly painted or
papered walls.

DOUBLING WEALTH IN THE
DINING ROOM

The best method for symbolically
doubling the family wealth is to place a
full-size mirror on one wall of the
dining room. When the mirror reflects
food on the dining table it is said to be
most auspicious.

DINING TABLES

These should be round, oval or square,
though round is best as this shape not
only represents the metal element – in
this case gold – signifying prosperity
for the residents, but also unity. Tables
should seat six or eight.

THE MASTER BEDROOM

The feng shui of the master bedroom
exerts great influence over the marital
happiness of the couple. When the chi
of the bedroom is harmonious the
couple will enjoy a supportive and
successful relationship, and there will
be no separation or divorce.

REST AND RELAXATION

The energies in the bedroom should
be more yin than yang since a bedroom
which is too yang will cause its
residents to be overly active.
For this reason the bedroom should not
be activated with too many good
fortune symbols.

TABOOS IN THE BEDROOM: WATER

Although water brings wealth, it has no place in the bedroom, whether in the form of fishbowls and fountains or paintings of lakes and waterfalls. The colour blue, however, is acceptable, even though it represents water. Avoid black.

TABOOS IN THE BEDROOM: FLOWERS AND PLANTS

These are extremely yang and to be avoided. In a woman's bedroom they ruin romance luck, in a couple's they cause quarrels and infidelity. Flowers in the bedroom bring good luck only when recuperating from illness as they introduce yang energy into the room.

TABOOS IN THE BEDROOM: MIRRORS

If anything can wreck a marriage, it is
having a mirror facing the bed.
Mirrors in the bedroom, or indeed
anything with a reflective surface,
bring the entry of a third party into the
marriage. Cover televisions in the
bedroom with a screen before you
go to bed.

TABOOS IN THE BEDROOM:
OPEN SHELVES

Open bookshelves symbolize blades
cutting into you as you sleep, and it
can only be a matter of time before you
get sick. In fact open shelves are not
good feng shui anywhere. Have doors
fixed to the shelves or place books in
such a way that it nullifies the
blade effect.

IMPROVING YOUR LOVE
LIFE WITH FENG SHUI

Romance and love luck can be
improved by ensuring that the love
corner – the southwest – is energized
with the placement of auspicious
objects symbolizing marital bliss.
The best symbols to display for a great
love life are a pair of mandarin ducks,
or lovebirds.

FENG SHUI IN THE KITCHEN

Two opposing elements, water and fire,
interact here and feng shui in the
kitchen involves the correct balancing
of these two elements. Avoid
positioning the oven directly opposite
the sink or refrigerator, and do not
position the two elements too close to
one another.

KEEP REFRIGERATORS
WELL STOCKED

Having a well-stocked refrigerator –
the modern equivalent of the full rice
urn – at all times brings excellent
feng shui.

A FINAL WORD

Let the practice of feng shui be an
ongoing thing, stage by stage. Feng
shui is a powerful supplement to your
luck, but not a cure-all for everything.
Much of feng shui is a compromise –
let it be fun and you will easily benefit
from the luck of the earth.

The World of Feng Shui
online magazine is at:
http://www.wofs.com

Lillian Too's website is at:
http://www.lillian-too.com

Lillian Too's Jewellery site is at:
http//www.lilliantoojewellery.com

If you are interested in Buddhism,
please meet my lama at:
http//www.lamazopa.com